"Students hunger to know what the Bible says about the issues they struggle with every day. Teenagers also desperately want adults to shoot straight with them and treat them like the adults they are becoming. Tom Richards will be received and celebrated by the teenage community for doing just that! His honest look at culture and the pressures teenagers face, mixed with Scripture and practical, godly principles, have the potential to change lives and reclaim this generation for Jesus!"

Heather Flies, Junior High Pastor and Youth Communicator, Wooddale Church and Youth Specialties

"This book is written by a young man who really understands youth, culture, and ministry. Tom Richards' writing is very straightforward; it is full of sound biblical truth, replete with fresh/current illustrations, and laced with thought-provoking discussion questions. Read it. Use it. It will greatly enhance your insight and ministry effectiveness."

Troy Dobbs, Senior Pastor, Grace Church

"Tom has been working with students for over 20 years and knows them! More importantly, he knows the questions they are asking. If you have a high school or college student in your home, your church, or your school this book is a must read. It is a resource that you will use again and again!"

John Erwin, Founder, National Association of Family Ministries

"Between 13 and 30, young people solidify their beliefs and learn how to live. My heart beats to see them grow into two-handed warriors, equally trained in character and competence. I believe this book is a tool that will challenge them in that direction.

"Tom Richards has his finger on the pulse of today's youth and young adults. This book will serve as a guidepost on their Christian journey and help them bring faith to life. They will be challenged by the truth of God's Word and by real-life stories of young people who chose lives of global impact.

"Here's a book that will cause students and young adults to think about what you really believe and choose how you really want to live. "

Dr. Rick Mann, President, Crown College

DEVOTIONS
FOR REAL LIFE

summerside
PRESS™

Summerside Press, Inc.
Minneapolis 55438
www.summersidepress.com

iBelieve: Devotions for Real Life
Copyright © 2010 by Tom Richards

ISBN 978-1-935416-72-2

Cover and interior design by Studio Gear Box, www.studiogearbox.com
Cover photo by Matthias Clamer/Getty

Summerside Press™ is an inspirational publisher offering fresh,
irresistible books to uplift the heart and engage the mind.

Printed in China

To my mom, Carolyn, for raising me to know God personally and to know what I believe.

TABLE OF CONTENTS

DEVOTIONS

WEEK ONE

FOR REAL LIFE

what I believe about me

It seems that everyone has an opinion on how you should live your life, what you should do after school, what's important, and what's not. But what do you believe? Do you know? Have you really thought about it? Do you believe in God? Do you believe in heaven? Is hell for real, and if it is, what's so bad about it? Do you believe you should wait until marriage for sex? Do you believe that God made you on purpose and that He loves you right where you are?

You may know what you believe about some issues, but you have questions about others. Sometimes it helps to hear real stories of how others are dealing with the same issues. They may have you asking yourself questions about their situations. Once you start thinking about it, you may realize that you do indeed have a set of beliefs—even if you have never put them in a list or written them down.

iBelieve helps you walk through life right now. It gives you a place to think about what you believe and helps you form the beliefs that will set the foundation for your life.

Each week is broken down into five devotions. You can do one a day during the week. You can do them on weekends and take off the busy days in the middle of the week. It is flexible. Let it fit your schedule. At the end are questions to make you think, including some that are great to share with a group. So you and your friends can go through the devotions together if you want. Or you can make it part of your small group.

week one

The first week is all about discovering what you believe about *you*. Do you believe you are child of God? Made on purpose by God? Loved by Him? What do you believe about the talents He gave you? Are they yours to brag about or are they gifts to be thankful for? Do you know what it means to be a Christian? Do you believe you are a Christian? What you believe about you is the foundation for what you believe about the world around you, what you believe about God, and what you believe about eternity.

Take a week to read these real stories from real people and decide for yourself what you believe. At the end of each day's reading is a simple question to help you "own" your beliefs. Check the box when you know what you believe. If you aren't sure, keep on digging to bring the truth of God's Word into your heart.

WEEK1 //DAY1
CHICKEN

Eric tried cigarettes when he was ten because his friends tried them. At twelve, he smoked marijuana with an older cousin. By the time he started high school, he went "all the way" with a girl. His older brother loved to tell stories about his own sexual conquests—although most of his stories came from his imagination. But Eric wasn't afraid to try anything. His body was a roller coaster and he loved to chase the highest highs. One day, however, Eric's roller coaster reached the end of its track. Like a scene from *The*

Fast and the Furious, Eric ran his friend's car into a telephone pole while street racing. His friend nearly died. Both will live with mental and physical consequences from that race for the rest of their lives.

Eric seemed like a risk taker, an adrenaline chaser. But deep inside, he was really just a big chicken. Each thrill-seeking escapade was his attempt to impress someone else. He was always afraid he wasn't enough. He was scared he was unlovable. He feared he didn't measure up to his friends, cousin, brother, or anyone else.

If only Eric would have had the perspective he has today. Now, as a young man in his twenties, Eric knows he is a child of God. He finds comfort in knowing he's made by God and known by God. That knowledge gives him self-confidence. He no longer worries about fitting in or measuring up to other people's standards.

we are transparent

God knows our thoughts—every dream, desire, feeling, and

insecurity. We can't hide anything from God. He knows things about us that we don't know about ourselves. The Bible says He even knows the number of our days and exactly how many hairs are on each of our heads.

If God knows all the bad stuff about us, how will we ever measure up?

Since we're so transparent to God, He knows everything good *and* He knows all of our sin. He knows every:
- evil thought
- bit of jealousy
- lustful desire
- critical thought
- prideful attitude
- cruel word
- dishonest act

Here's the deal: God loves us in spite of our sin. Knowing God loves us just as we are is an empowering truth to cling to. In Eric's case, he didn't need to work so hard and act so careless to get people to approve of him when he was growing up. He didn't need to be so afraid that he wouldn't measure up. All along, God loved him just as he was. He was a child of God. And so are you!

Some people have wonderful parents on earth and others wish they did. In either case, God is our perfect Father. He is always strong, always loving, and always there. And we are always His children.

god Loves us too much

He loves us just the way we are but *too much* to let us stay that way.

Great parents act the same way. They love their children at every age, but they always desire for their children to mature. Nobody wants to raise a spoiled, bratty kid who throws tantrums in public or gets into trouble with the law. Good parents work hard to help their kids grow up.

"God knows our thoughts—every dream, desire, feeling, and insecurity. We can't hide anything from God. He knows things about us that we don't know about ourselves."

God is the best parent of them all. He's our Father in heaven and He knows us by name. God will give us every opportunity to grow and mature into a Christ-follower—no need to try to impress Him or work hard to be accepted. He loves us unconditionally through every step of our Christian journey. He loves us enough to give us boundaries and allow us to face consequences. And He loves us enough to call us His children.

iThink

1. Describe a situation when you felt as though you didn't measure up. What did you do to compensate for that feeling? _____

_____

_____

_____

2. How does it make you feel knowing God knows everything about you and loves you anyway? _____

_____

_____

3. What does it mean to say "God loves me just as I am but too much to let me stay that way"? _____

_____

_____

_____

4. Describe what it means that God is our Father in heaven.

_____

_____

_____

_____

_____

_____

_____

_____

_____

_____

_____

_____

Check here if you believe that you are a child of God.

WEEK1 // DAY2
CRAZY LOVE

iBelieve in God's unconditional love

A newspaper once reported that a man loved his Cadillac so much he decided to have it buried next to him when he died. A story has also been told that a millionaire loved her dog so much she willed her entire estate to the dog when she died—complete with butler, maid, and doggie chef. What's more, one man almost lost his life running back into his burning house to retrieve his beloved college football trophy. Love can be a weird thing.

I've only had one brand new car in my life—a fine-tuned, sporty, German-built machine. I *loved* my car. I loved it, that is, until my I got my third speeding ticket and my insurance went through the roof. The next week, I traded my love in for an old Ford.

Love can be crazy. It seems to come and go. Sometimes it's hard to know what love is. Maybe that's because there are three different kinds of love…and only one of them is guaranteed to ALWAYS be there for you.

Friendship Love

Marcus is one of my best friends. I absolutely love spending time with him. I have the deepest respect for my friend because he is one of the most devoted Christ-followers I know. Even so, I still screw up when it comes to treating Marcus with the love of Christ that's in me. Selfishness, impatience, and pride get the best of me and I fall short of being an unconditionally loving friend.

Even the best, best friends in the world are selfish sometimes. Have you ever had your feelings hurt by a friend, intentionally or unintentionally? Of course—we all have! Some friendships grow and some friendships break. The friendship kind of love is wonderful, but it sometimes fails.

Some crazy fans fall in love with movie stars they've never met. Junior high kids fall in love with their secret crushes, if only for a moment in time.

ROMANTIC LOVE

Some people say that Valentine's Day is a holiday invented by greeting card and chocolate companies. Valentine's Day is a big money maker because there is a part in all of us that desires to be in love.

Even people who truly fall in love treat each other in unloving ways sometimes. In fact, some statistics suggest that fifty percent of marriages end in divorce because people say they've fallen *out* of love.

My grandma and grandpa were married sixty years— a very long time! But four years ago, my grandma died, leaving my grandpa heartbroken. In even the most committed marriages, loved ones die, leaving a gaping hole in the other's heart.

Romantic love is an amazing experience, but at some point—in a moment of failure, in separation or divorce, or ultimately in death—romantic love fails too.

"There is one kind of love that never fails."

unconditional love

Love without conditions comes only from God. This type of love is not about a feeling, it's about a choice. God chooses to love us all the time. He also calls us to exercise our choice to act in a loving way to others, including our enemies. In other words, even when we don't have a *good feeling* about someone else, we are still called to show love to that person. So what does that look like? What does that mean?

In the Bible, 1 Corinthians 13:4–8 paints a clear picture of unconditional love. Can you fill in the blanks below? (Try it before checking your answers at the bottom.)

"Love is patient, love is _____. It does not envy, it does not boast, it is not _____. It is not _____, it is not self-seeking, it is not easily _____, it keeps no record of wrongs. Love does not delight in evil but rejoices with the truth. It always protects, always trusts, always hopes, always perseveres. Love never _____."

There is nothing we can do to make God love us more, and there is nothing we can do to make Him love us less. God loves us unconditionally. Even when He is disappointed by our choices or hurt by our sins, He chooses to love us. How much does God love us? John 3:16 says God loves us so much He sent His son Jesus to die for our sins.

Now, that's crazy love!

(Fill-in-the-blank answers for 1 Corinthians 13:4–8: kind, proud, rude, angered, fails.)

ithink

1. Who is the last person you had a crush on? What did you love about that person? _____

_____

_____

_____

2. Who is the hardest person to show love to? Why? ____

_____

_____

3. Describe a personal experience that seemed like unconditional love until it disappointed you. _____

_____

_____

4. Do you really believe that God loves you no matter what? Why or why not? _____

_____

_____

⬤   Check here if you believe that God loves you unconditionally.

WEEK1 // DAY3
A MASTERPIECE

Oprah Winfrey interviewed the most famous supermodel of them all—one of the most beautiful women in the entire world. The audience gasped and viewers at home were amazed when Oprah asked the model if there were any parts of her body she wished she could change. Without pause to consider the question, the model replied yes—and then proceeded to list all the parts of her body she wished were different.

If one of the world's best-known supermodels feels that way about herself, it's probably safe to say that most of us feel the same way. However, Ephesians 2:10 says we are God's workmanship. Look it up! He made our bodies and they are works of art. The Bible tells us our bodies are temples built by God. We are important just as we are. If you believe that's true, it will change how you view your body.

With the idea that God designed and put us together Himself, finish these thoughts:

• Something unique about me is: _____
_____ .

• My best feature is: _____ .

• God really had a sense of humor when He gave me: _____
_____ .

• It's probably silly that I spend so much time worrying about my:_____ .

• Knowing I am God's workmanship without any mistakes makes me feel:_____ .

No Mistakes

Jessica and Ryan are brother and sister. She thinks she's too tall and he thinks he's too short. Each wish they could trade a few inches with the other to become the perfect height. Debbie and Diane are friends who joke that if they could just trade some fat—one wants more and one wants less—they'd have perfect bodies. You probably have ideas of ways your body would look better—if only God cared enough to listen to you. Well, He does.

God wants us to believe that He made no mistakes in creating us. Each of us has the voice, hair color, eyes, and nose He chose for us. In fact, God not only chose the genes we were born with—he did so perfectly. Each time we bash ourselves for not looking a certain way, we criticize the very masterpiece God is perfecting in us each day. When we accept ourselves for the work of art that He made, we offer worship to Him.

Masterpiece

It took Michelangelo four years to paint the scenes on the ceiling of the Sistine Chapel. Da Vinci took just as long to complete his Mona Lisa portrait. These works of art were labors of love for their famous creators. The original sketches could have stood alone as great works of art, but after four years of perfecting, the final pieces were true masterpieces.

God created us when He gave us life—we were amazing then. But we are His *masterpieces* every day of our lives. He never stops perfecting us. Like the process of creating a masterpiece, God adds strokes of genius as a painter would and chisels away raw imperfections as a sculptor would. He refines us, His masterpieces, into something perfect in His sight.

Beyond Beauty

God formed you in your mother's womb like he formed no other. It goes way beyond physical appearances. Your natural personality, preferences, and quirks are all part of the original design. It's funny to see that even as babies we each have a unique personality. God didn't do this just because He's creative—He made you so He can delight in you! He made you to do good works with your natural gifts

Only God's power could create something as beautiful and complex as the human body. Standard with every model you'll find:
- eyes that blink.
- a heart that beats.
- lungs that breathe.
- teeth that chew.
- laughter that erupts from within.
- tears that flow.

What other attributes would you add?

- _____
- _____

and abilities. He made you to reflect His power and beauty through your life.

As amazing as it is that our lungs breathe on autopilot, it's just as amazing that there are six billion people (and counting) on earth, and there are no two alike! God made us to be biological miracles and unique works of art at the same time. So how does it feel to be a masterpiece?

iThink

1. Why is it hard to think of yourself as God's workmanship? _____

_____

2. How does the idea that God made you without any mistakes make you feel about wanting to change the way you are made? _____

_____

_____

_____

3. What does your relationship with God the Creator have to do with your self-image? _____

_____

_____

_____

4. Describe something about the way God made you that you will begin to embrace rather than regret. _____

_____

_____

_____

_____

 Check here if you believe that you are one of God's masterpieces.

WEEK1 //DAY4
NOT SO BAD...

Pride hurts. It hurts us and it hurts others. Trent learned that lesson the hard way.

Trent played high school football. He was a star player on his team—one of the very best in the school. And he knew it! Trent not only knew how good he was, he knew how much better he was than everyone else. So he told them, often. He had a special knack for putting down guys who tried hard but lacked natural talent. He relished being the best.

When Trent went out for the football team at a Big East Conference university, his dreams of playing college football came to an end. Trent didn't even make the team as a walk-on player. Quite simply, he wasn't good enough at a big school. His confidence came from his ability to be a star, and when his days as a star ended, Trent was depressed and broken.

Trent's problem was that he gave himself way too much credit when he was a star athlete. He thought his natural talent was somehow his doing. It never dawned on him to give God the recognition for his talent and to walk through the halls at school with a little humility.

Most of us are like Trent on some level. We're never as good as we think we are but we're also never as bad as we think we are. Whether we're self-loving or self-loathing, pride is at work. When life is going great, we take way too much credit. And when life gets tough, our pride is hurt and we are embarrassed—another way of taking too much credit.

Marty's sign

Marty has a sign over his desk that says "Pride is contending for supremacy with God." Pride is taking credit that's due to God and failing to acknowledge dependence on Him. God hates pride. It's not hard to see why.

Last Christmas I gave my grandparents a fantastic present—two tickets for an all-expense-paid weekend getaway at a resort. The next week, they sent my brother a thank you note for the big gift—the gift from ME! Two weeks later, they sent a postcard from the resort again thanking my brother for such a generous gift. It drove me crazy that they did not remember the true source of their gift.

God doesn't like it when we mistake His work for our own, just as I didn't like it when my grandparents mistook my gift for my brother's. His work includes our natural abilities and talents—after all, He created us. His work includes every blessing and good fortune that comes our way. Everything good comes from God, but we so often take credit for His work. We let pride take over.

As much as we may hate the worst of the worst, we hate nothing as much as God hates pride. He hates pride so much because it's in direct opposition to Him.

God hates pride. What do you hate?
- I hate racism
- I hate child abuse
- I hate poverty
- I hate terrorism
- I hate incurable diseases
- _____
- _____
- _____

Give credit where credit is Due

One of the most successful recording artists of all time has sold nearly 200 million albums worldwide. She's also won more awards than any other female artist in history. Every time she takes the stage to receive an award—before big stars and televised audiences of millions—she gives credit first and foremost to her "Lord and Savior, Jesus Christ." She knows the source of her talent and gives credit where credit is due.

In our weakest moments God shows us grace and mercy. And in our best moments He should get the glory. If we

remember that we are neither as good nor as bad as we
imagine, we can concentrate on God's gifts and defeat pride.

iThink

1. Tell of a time when you took too much credit for
something God did in or through you. Why do you feel you
took too much credit? _____

_____

_____

_____

_____

2. Why do you think we swing like a pendulum, from
thinking too highly of ourselves to thinking we're no good
at all? _____

_____

_____

_____

_____

3. Who is a great example of humility in your life? _____

_____

_____

_____

4. Identify an area of pride that's lingering in your life, and why it's harmful. If you can't think of one, ask someone in your group if they see an area of pride in your life. _____

_____

_____

_____

_____

_____

_____

_____

_____

_____

_____

Check here if you believe that pride is contending for supremacy with God.

WEEK1//DAY5
JOHN'S 180

John was a stand-out guy in his youth group. He was part of the student leadership team, went on mission trips around the world, sang in the youth choir, and never missed a camp or retreat. He was a fantastic example for younger students to look up to—everybody respected John and noticed his godly example.

In college, John changed into someone new at warp speed. By the end of the first term, he had turned into the typical wild-frat-boy-wearing-a-toga image portrayed in movies. Today, one-night stands, casual sex, beer, and bongs are as much a part of John's life as God seemed to be back in high school. John's 180-degree-turn for the worse has destroyed some of his most cherished relationships and broken trust with his family. Even more disturbing, John has become distant from God.

Is John still a Christian? Was he ever a Christian? Are his experiences with God as a teenager good enough to make him a Christian today? Even he wonders.

John had wonderful experiences in his youth group growing up, but those experiences alone don't mean he's a Christian. Going to church doesn't make you a Christian any more than standing in a garage makes you a car. Just believing in God doesn't make you a Christian either—the Devil himself believes in God and he's certainly not a Christian! And it doesn't matter if your parents are Christians. God has no grandchildren, just children! The only way to become a Christian—a follower of Jesus—is to invite Him into your life once and for all.

Ben

Ben played college football and met weekly with the Fellowship of Christian Athletes group on campus. He was as nice as they come. Ben never took the 180-degree-turn John took in college, yet a friend asked Ben if he thought of himself as a Christian. The reason the friend asked was because Ben didn't show outward signs of a personal relationship with Jesus. He wasn't seen reading his Bible or sharing his faith. If he was a Christian, shouldn't it show?

In the Bible, the Book of Matthew says we'll know a tree by its fruit. If a tree grows apples, it's definitely an apple tree, (not an orange tree, or plum tree, or walnut tree). When a person becomes a Christian,

Signs of life as a Christian include:

- inviting Jesus to be your Savior
- beginning to love what God loves
- beginning to hate what God hates
- surrendering to God (not trying to control everything)
- caring about where friends will spend eternity
- trusting that God forgives and loves unconditionally

there will be signs of new life growing from that relationship with Jesus just like fruit grows from a tree.

SO HOW DO YOU KNOW IF YOU KNOW GOD?

When I was a little kid, there was a boy on my block nobody liked. My mom made me invite him to my fifth birthday party. I cried every step of the way to his house. At his door, with red puffy eyes and snot running from my nose, I reluctantly invited the twerp to my party, fully believing he was going to suck all the fun out of my big day. I genuinely did not want him to attend.

When we invite God into our lives, He knows whether we're genuinely ready to surrender, or merely reciting words from a prayer. He searches our hearts and sees our motives. Becoming a Christian is not just fire insurance against hell; it's a decision to follow God beginning now and renewing that commitment every day.

If you've never genuinely invited Jesus into your life to forgive you of your sin and be your Lord, you can right now. There is no official prayer. Simply, in your own words:

- Thank God for sending His son Jesus to die for your sins.
- Admit you are a sinner living a sinful life.
- Ask Jesus to come into your life and forgive your sins.
- Ask Jesus to take control of your life.
- Tell Jesus you believe that He's in you and will never leave you.

Even if it is the simplest of prayers, this prayer can have a profound impact on your life.

Are you ready for a 180?

iThink

1. Describe a time in your life when you "went through the motions" but were faking it. ——————————

———————————————————————

———————————————————————

2. How does the biblical illustration of knowing a tree by its fruit apply to Christians today? _____

_____

_____

_____

_____

3. Can you point to any spiritual "fruit" in your life—any outward evidence of new life in Jesus? _____

_____

_____

_____

_____

4. Is there anything holding you back from giving your life to Jesus or living your life for Him? _____

_____

_____

_____

_____

_____

Check here if you believe you are a Christian.

DEVOTIONS

WEEK TWO

FOR REAL LIFE

hat I Believe about christian Living

Have you ever heard of an aspiring basketball player passing up a chance to play for an NBA team because there were just too many rules? No way—the NBA is the pinnacle experience for any athlete with a passion for basketball. But did you know that along with fame and fortune, joining a professional sports franchise requires sacrifice too?

Built into every professional athlete's contract are requirements for training, practice, and schedules. Beyond those, there are requirements that spell out what each player *can't* do—like snowboarding! Once a team invests so much into a player, they need to protect him from twisting an ankle or getting a concussion when not on the court. The player has a choice: play in the NBA or snowboard and take a chance on never playing professionally again. It's usually an easy decision!

Living the Christian life is all about following your passion for God. The person without passion will see the Bible as a bunch of rules meant to suck the fun out of life. The person with passion for God will see that there's no better way to walk through life than by following the guidelines from God's Word.

A wise man once told me, "The reward for living the Christian life isn't heaven. Heaven is a free gift from God. The reward for living the Christian life is *living* the Christian life!" The best part of living for God is that it's all about a personal relationship with Him. It's not about religion or rules.

In Week Two, we'll explore some really interesting ideas. For starters, do you believe fear can be a bad thing AND a good thing?

Also, we'll consider this: Perhaps the greatest impact on our relationship with God is the company we keep. In Christian-talk, we call it "community." The Bible tells us to surround ourselves with others who also follow God.

Living a life for God includes making tough choices. What's harder for you? Sharing your stuff or obeying churchy rules? Sharing and obeying are tied closely to your faith. Discover why they are important to the Christian life.

There is always a way out of even the most tempting situations. It's a promise from God. In this chapter we learn how having faith can get us through the most trying times.

You're off to a great start in the *iBelieve* journey. As you formulate what you believe, why not experience God in a new way and put your faith into action right now?

iBelieve I should fear God

Fear can be a bad thing, like when little kids are so afraid of the dark they'd rather pee in bed than walk to the bathroom. But it can be a good thing too, like when you buckle your seatbelt because you're afraid of flying through the windshield in a car accident. Sometimes, fear works to our advantage because it keeps us from harm.

It's also good to fear God, but not like we fear a big bully. By interchanging the words *no* and *know* from the phrase "Know

God, No Fear", we can better understand the awesomeness of fearing God. In the following paragraphs, notice how each exchange alters the meaning of the phrase, and helps make sense of what it really means to be in awe of God.

Know God, Know Fear

If you were invited to the White House to meet the president of the United States, you'd probably be at least a little nervous. Maybe even a lot nervous! But why? There's no reason to be afraid. He's not going to make fun of you. He certainly won't hit you or kick you. There may be a better word than *fear* to describe the nervousness: *respect*. Maybe even *awe*. Americans hold a healthy respect, or reverence, for the office of the president. Now think about God. He has way more power than the leaders of all the countries on earth—combined. And we can approach Him whenever we want.

To fear the Lord, from a biblical perspective, is to actually *feel* respect for God. It's to be so in awe of God that we never get numb to the idea that He is God! Fear of the Lord is an attitude of respect backed up by actions that demonstrate respect.

Jesse is reckless and out of control. Financially unstable, emotionally unavailable, and deeply insecure, he is leaving a wake of destruction behind him. Jesse's risky behavior has landed him in jail, has caused broken trust with everyone in his life, and has stunted his ability to develop emotionally from teenager to adult.

In a moment of honesty, Jesse admitted he's just waiting for something really bad to happen. So far, the consequences haven't hit him hard enough. An unplanned child or life-long disease may be the wake-up call he's waiting for.

Jesse is living his life without God and without fear of God. Since he does not respect God, he does not know how to respect himself. Without God there is no fear of consequences, no fear of an eternity without Him, no fear of destructive behaviors. Without God people feel miserable, lost, and lonely.

No God, Know Fear

Ashley was put in an ambulance with large cuts on her neck, wrists, and legs. Just before this, she had a fight with her dad and then had run away with a razorblade in her hand. She started cutting herself as she ran from the house in the dank, dark night. She was found by strangers, lying on the ground in a public park, crying and shaking.

It wasn't the first time Ashley had done something like that. She has struggled since her mom died, reacting with dramatic emotions and often running away. She sometimes says she prefers to be in treatment facilities because she feels safer and less stressed there. Yet, no matter how many times she goes to treatment programs, she repeats her behavior once she is released.

Ashley feels rejected by her family and all alone in life. Sometimes she's so scared she actually hurts herself in a cry for help. Ashley has no God in her life, and she knows fear. Without God, life is scary and uncertain.

Know God, No Fear

Knowing God is putting your trust in Him. Trust that He loves you and will provide for your every need. When we know God, we know Him like a personal friend. We have no reason to be scared of God. God is for us! He will never leave us. Having "fear" of the Lord is the same as having "deep respect." Because of who He is, we have every reason to feel respect for Him and show it in the way that we live. We no longer fear the unknown, fear the future, or fear our circumstances.

As we come to know Him as our personal Savior, we never need to be afraid of:
- loneliness (John 14:18)
- dying (Revelation 21:4)
- illness (Jeremiah 17:4)
- Satan (Romans 16:20)
- financial troubles (Psalm 113:7)
- rejection (Isaiah 41:9)

1. How would you describe a biblical fear of the Lord to someone? _____

_____

_____

2. What are some examples of healthy fear or respect that keeps you safe? (Fear of an accident helps keep drivers safe, etc.) _____

_____

_____

3. Which of the four sections above do you relate to the most right now? _____

_____

_____

4. Do you think most Christians in America have a biblical fear of God? Who do you know who does? _____

_____

_____

Check here if you believe you should fear God.

WEEK2//DAY2
SIDE-BY-SIDE

If you knew Reid in high school, he'd be your friend. He was the kind of guy everyone wanted to be friends with: good looking, smart, funny, and athletic—but most of all, he was an all-around good guy.

Reid earned a nickname for himself among his friends at school: Root Beer Boy. Each week, when his friends would drink alcohol at parties, Reid brought his own bottles of root beer. By default, he was the designated driver because he was usually the only one sober at the end of the night. He took pride in being the good guy.

After graduating from high school and moving to a Christian college, Reid's perspective changed. Playing football on a team of Christians, he found himself surrounded by peers who loved God more than he ever did. Where he once thought he was at the top of his Christian walk, he realized he was still back toward the very beginning. He said, "In high school, I used to think I was the best. Once I got to college I realized I was just the best of the worst."

Reid's experience isn't that rare. Until faced with real temptations and challenges, students' faith can stall, without them even knowing it. In college, Reid found three types of relationships every Christian needs to experience: people who offer a hand to help you, people who need a hand to help them, and people who grow alongside you. Imagine climbing the rungs of a ladder. As you are offered a hand up, or reach down to offer your own hand, your Christian faith grows in new ways.

up the Ladder

Finding a faith mentor—someone with more wisdom and commitment to the Lord in their Christian walk—will challenge you and pull you up. It will happen much the way a coach trains an athlete. Can you picture a Little League team of ten-year-olds coaching themselves? They would probably lose every game of the season without the wisdom and expertise of a seasoned coach. Don't merely self-coach. Pursue the wisdom and example of men and women who love God and care about you.

Down the Ladder

Focus on someone *you* can mentor—someone you can challenge in his or her faith. You don't need to be at the pinnacle of the Christian faith (there is no such thing, by the way) to help someone else grow. You just need to be a few rungs ahead with wisdom God has taught you through experience. Reaching out to help someone else grow develops a different part of your faith than taking a hand offered to you.

side-by-side

Relationships of accountability can spur others around you to live for God. Standing strong for something that matters to God encourages someone else who's trying to stand strong. Nothing can replace community—or coming together—with other Christians. We're made to cheer each other on and sharpen each other as iron sharpens iron.

All these types of relationships are necessary to develop our faith. In Reid's life, it was not until he found them that his faith truly came alive. He went from being a stagnant Christian to a fully-devoted Christian. Today he is surrounded by the best friends anyone could ask for—friends who challenge him in different ways. He is passionate about using his gifts and talents to bring honor to God and he's genuinely happy living such a purposeful, rich life. You can be too!

"As you are offered a hand up, or reach down to offer your own hand, your Christian faith grows in new ways."

1. Who has encouraged you as a Christian more than anyone else? How has this person pointed you toward God? _____

_____

_____

_____

2. Name one person in your life who will tell you when you're wrong. _____

_____

_____

_____

3. On the ladder of Christian growth, where do you need God's guidance most: helping others, asking for help, or climbing side-by-side with a friend? _____

_____

_____

_____

_____

_____

4. Do you relate more to Reid's high school or college experience? Explain. _____

_____

_____

_____

_____

_____

_____

_____

_____

_____

_____

_____

_____

_____

_____

_____

_____

_____

Check here if you believe godly relationships are necessary.

WEEK2//DAY3
MY $TUFF

Scott and Lisa teach me a lot about "stuff." Actually, they model the right way to think about *their* stuff and I learn from their great example. They have a big house, a nice cabin, and a condo in Florida, and each is stocked full of fun stuff.

They have:

- a bowling alley
- jet skis
- home theaters
- a juke box

- a hot tub and sauna

- bumper cars

- a zip line in the woods

- hidden doors behind bookshelves that lead to
  secret rooms (for real!)

These people share everything they have! Every winter
and spring, dozens of family members, friends, and even
strangers spend vacation in paradise because Scott and Lisa
share their beach condo. Small and large groups of students
go to their cabin for wakeboarding weekends. Once, I even
threw a New Year's Eve party in their main home while they
were out of town (and they knew about it!).

Scott will tell you that he's lucky to be blessed with "stuff."
But he says it doesn't do anyone any good if it just sits
around collecting dust. So he shares everything. Lisa has a
special gift of creating a warm and comfortable environment,
so guests feel at home. Together, they are terrific stewards!

what's a steward?

A steward is someone who manages something that is not his own. Scott and Lisa believe what the Bible teaches about the source of all of their stuff. It's not theirs because of hard work and smart investing, although both are important. God has entrusted them to manage the resources that He has allowed them to receive.

"Everything we receive ultimately comes from God."

Just like Scott and Lisa, everything we receive ultimately comes from God. Our hard work merely exercises the abilities and talents God endowed us with. We are told in 1 Chronicles 29:11–14 that everything we have is really God's—we're just the managers of His resources.

sharing

Joey used to ask his parents for gift cards to restaurants in $10 increments so he would not feel obligated to buy a friend's meal with his gift. But eventually he realized that being cheap is stressful. Waiters say that when college friends go out to restaurants for late night snacks, their pooled cash never quite covers the bill and tip. Everyone is so tight with their money. Sharing what you have, even when it isn't much, not only fulfills your responsibility to God, but brings joy to you and others.

Five easy ways to start sharing:

1. When going on a trip to the beach or an outdoor event, bring enough snacks to share.

2. For every new shirt or pair of jeans you buy, give an old one away. Keep the same number of hangers and just rotate the old clothes out as the new comes in.

3. When you are lucky enough to have a place of your own, offer soda and snacks to your guests. It's fun to be a generous host (and your place will become the cool hangout).

4. Do something nice for a friend who drives you around. Pay for a car wash, grab a coffee, or offer to pay for gas.

5. Serve someone a dose of generosity instead of a bill for service. Mow a lawn, babysit, help someone move or paint, and don't ask for a dime.

Nobody likes a tightwad, yet we all fall victim to being cheap from time to time. Strive to create an environment of generosity among your circle of friends. It may turn into a contest to see who can be the most generous! And the great thing is, you all become good stewards.

1. Describe the most generous person in your life. _____

_____

_____

_____

_____

2. Describe a time when it was easy for you to be generous.

_____

_____

_____

_____

3. What's one situation where it's challenging for you to share or be generous? _____

_____

_____

_____

_____

4. Write down one or two of your own ideas of easy ways to start sharing. _____

_____

_____

_____

_____

_____

_____

_____

_____

_____

_____

● Check here if you believe that your "stuff" belongs to God.

iBelieve in obedience to God

Most people don't like rules. Rules seem to take the fun out of life. Most people I know want to try something even more when they're told not to.

Alcohol has never been part of my life. It tastes like poison and costs more than soda. I never drink because, as a youth leader, I know how important my example is to young eyes. And the best part is, I know I'm not missing anything. I'm glad to not drink. But the minute my church made a rule that banned staff from consuming alcohol, guess what I wanted to do? You guessed it—I wanted to drink alcohol! For many Christians (young and old), the Bible seems like a bunch of old rules that only exist to suck the fun out of life. Once we know of a rule, it becomes alluring to consider breaking it. But there's another way to see it.

Consider a train. When it's on tracks, it's strong and powerful. It's fast and can go long distances. Trains sometimes seem unstoppable. But a train without a track isn't strong, powerful, or fast. It can't go anywhere. It isn't unstoppable—it's stuck.

Think of the Bible as tracks that will:

- serve as boundaries to keep you safe
- keep you on course and moving in the right direction
- give you momentum and strength
- allow you to tap into the power of God Himself
- keep you from getting stuck

God is our Creator; He knows best how this thing called life works. The sooner we come into agreement with that, the sooner we'll discover the best life possible. And the way to come into agreement with that is through obedience.

pete Loses His Faith

Pete and his girlfriend were sexually active. As a junior in high school, Pete stopped living for God and started living for himself in the area of sexual purity. Pete lost his faith… at least in that area of his life.

Pete's behavior screamed that he was not going to follow God's way. He didn't believe God's way was best for him. He didn't believe he was hurting himself or his girlfriend. Pete chose a sexual relationship with someone outside of marriage when he knew it was against God's Word. Because he was intent on living for himself, Pete started making more and more decisions that were against God and the Bible. One area of disobedience led to disobedience in other areas. Pretty soon his life fell apart.

obedience Recognizes authority

Imagine the audacity of a person who visits a restaurant, but instead of waiting for the server, enters the kitchen and cooks his own meal. He'd be thrown out of the restaurant because he never had the authority to enter the kitchen. How about a guy who walks into a bank, but rather than waiting in line, goes behind the counter to withdraw money himself? He'd be arrested on the spot, regardless of the money he had in his account. It's a matter of authority. When God demands our obedience and takes careful attention to leave us an entire book of instructions, it's in our best interest to obey. It's a matter of authority. Nobody knows better than the Inventor how the invention works best. You and I are God's ideas.

> "God is our creator;
> He knows best how this thing
> called life works."

Don't be fooled—obedience to God will never cost you one bit of fun in life. When you choose to obey God, all you lose is unnecessary strife and pain. Sin always brings consequences, and it always complicates things. Sin keeps you from God. But obedience lays tracks to bring you closer to Him.

1. What's the dumbest rule you had to obey growing up?

_____

_____

_____

_____

_____

2. What's one rule your parents had that you'll use with your own kids one day? _____

_____

_____

_____

_____

_____

3. Describe one time it felt really good to do the right thing.

_____

_____

_____

_____

_____

_____

_____

_____

4. Describe one area of your life where you feel off-track.

What can you do to get back on track? _____

_____

_____

_____

_____

_____

_____

_____

_____

Check here if you believe you should be obedient
to God.

WEEK2//DAY5
ALWAYS

Rain will always come right after a car wash. Tourists will always drive slowly. Americans will always speak loudly to people who don't understand English (as if talking LOUDER will make them understand). Outside of these obvious certainties, it's hard to bank on something so steady that it will always occur. But God promises a big always: He will always provide an escape from temptation to sin. ALWAYS.

A combustible combination

Our sin nature and Satan's mission to tempt us with sin is a combustible combination. As human beings, we have an appetite for sin and the Devil knows it.

Satan takes great pleasure in tempting Christians to sin. He may lose the war when we become Christians, but he wants to win some battles by tangling us in a web of sin. If he can distract us for even a moment, it's a moment our eyes are off of God. The more he bogs us down in sin, the less of a threat we are to promote Christ to others.

Always a way out

As a teenager, Sarah worked at a retail store and quickly learned that shoplifting does not officially occur until the culprit exits the store. One time she noticed a man sneak a pair of shoes into his bag. The store policy was to give the would-be crook every opportunity to pay before walking out the door and officially becoming a criminal.

First, Sarah made it clear she was watching. She walked right up to the man and said, "I saw you shopping over near the shoes. Did you find your size?" He seemed unfazed and continued to linger around the store. When he finally approached the exit he had one more chance. Sarah asked the man if there was anything he wanted to pay for. He said, "No, I couldn't find anything today." And as soon as he stepped out of the door, he was arrested by the mall police.

We are like that man who was caught shoplifting when we make a bad decision or get into a bad situation and refuse opportunities to make it right. Once that happens, it can feel like there's no going back. But God says there is always a way out of sinning against Him, no matter what the temptation or situation.

We will never face temptation beyond what we can handle (1 Corinthians 10:13). We will never be pushed past our limit. Sometimes the escape is right in front of our eyes, and other times we need to stop and look for it. It will always be there.

NO EXCUSES

Next time you're tempted to go against God's way, cling to His promise and look for a way out of the situation.

D. L. Moody, the founder of Moody Bible Institute in Chicago, used to say, "Sin will keep you from the Bible, or the Bible will keep you from sin." He was right.

It's simply not true to say "I couldn't help it," or "I couldn't stop." Where there is dangerous temptation on the Christian road, there is always a safe lane for passing. You always have a choice.

Ways to avoid temptation:
- Pray and ask God to show you a way out of the situation.
- Find someone else and be strong together.
- Open your Bible and find truth to combat the lies.
- Turn to a trusted mentor or adult and ask for help.
- Draw strength from another time when God helped you withstand temptation.

1. James 4:7 says "Resist the devil and he will flee from you." What is an example of this playing out in your life?

_____

_____

_____

_____

_____

2. Describe a time when it seemed like there was no way to avoid a temptation to sin. _____

_____

_____

_____

_____

3. Can you now think of a way out of that temptation? ___

_____

_____

_____

_____

_____

4. Next time you feel trapped, like there is no way out of the trouble you are about to enter, what will you do? _____

_____

_____

_____

_____

_____

_____

_____

_____

_____

_____

_____

_____

_____

_____

_____

_____

Check here if you believe God will always provide a way out of tough situations.

DEVOTIONS

WEEK THREE

FOR REAL LIFE

hat I believe about a godly Relationship

If I told you I knew a President of the United States personally, would you be impressed? I once worked for a presidential candidate during a really close election year. But here's the catch—he didn't know me. I was so low on the totem pole he wouldn't have even recognized my name. I didn't know him personally. I knew *of* him. I knew his voice, I knew his face, but I didn't know the man. And he didn't know me.

There is a life-changing, life-saving difference between knowing God personally and knowing *of* God. In the Bible, Matthew 7:21 and 23 says, "Not everyone who says to me 'Lord, Lord,' will enter the kingdom of heaven.... I will tell them plainly, 'I never knew you.'"

Religion turns a lot of people away from God. It's not a good thing when religious traditions and legalism distract us from the God who is calling out to us. But being a Christian isn't about dedication to a religion. Being a Christian is about knowing God *personally*.

God wants you to know Him as personally as He knows you. He craves a genuine relationship with you. What does that look like? In many ways, it takes the same effort other relationships take. People don't become best friends without talking to each other, without spending time together, without getting to know each other. You can't grow closer without investing in the relationship.

That's how it works with God too. He didn't make us robots, pre-programmed to love Him and follow Him. He gave us free will and leaves it to us to choose to spend time with Him. That way it's genuine. That way it's a real relationship.

Week Three is a journey of growing in our relationship with God. Here are some tough questions you may have asked about what you believe:

- When I pray, does God hear me?
- Why read the Bible? Isn't it just a bunch of old stories?
- How do I "hear" God?
- What do my talents have to do with God?
- Why would I tell other people what I believe about God?

As you contemplate your relationship with God, do you want to know *of* God (like someone you've heard of) or know God...*personally*? The relationship you build is up to you and what you believe.

WEEK3//DAY1
EMERGENCY 911

I used to think of God as a great contact in case of emergencies—sort of like a 911 call.

Once, late at night, I was running around Lake Harriet in the middle of Minneapolis. It's a beautiful trail, but after midnight, it's pretty secluded and scary. I was about halfway around the lake when I heard a noise from behind me that sounded like chains. My mind started to race, and after a few minutes I was convinced a serial killer was chasing me. I knew with certainty that he'd use the chain to strangle me.

In desperation, I prayed to God and asked Him to protect me from danger. Just as I finished praying, I grasped my chest and stopped running, completely out of breath. The noise from behind stopped. I felt something under my shirt—it was a metal whistle I still had around my neck from lifeguarding earlier in the day. It rattled as I ran, so I literally was running from myself the entire time! At that moment, I felt conviction in my heart. God had become my 911 operator. It had been days or weeks since I talked to Him outside of an emergency.

Relying on God for emergencies *only* is like using a car to only listen to the radio. Once I caught my breath that night, I prayed a real prayer to God—an ACTS prayer. The acronym ACTS helps me remember that the Bible teaches us to pray full, real prayers.

Adoration (praising God for who He is)

Confession (confessing our sins and asking for forgiveness)

Thanksgiving (thanking God for His blessings)

Supplication (asking God to work and believing He's able)

Here's a challenge: take two minutes right now and pray your own ACTS prayer to God.

For many people God is like their:

- emergency contact (think 911)
- long-lost relative to call on Christmas and Easter
- push-button vending machine
- ATM or Bank
- genie in a bottle
- _____
- _____
- _____

Invest in a Relationship

Imagine if you only spoke to your parents every Christmas and Easter. What if you only talked to your best friends for twenty seconds at each meal, and then were silent the rest of the day? All relationships take time. Depth of relationship comes from spending time together and sharing life.

"Praying is one way to invest in your relationship with God."

Jeff, a high school guy, once challenged the idea of prayer. He said, "If God knows everything already, then why do I need to talk to Him? Does God really need my prayers?"

The answer is no. God does not need Jeff's prayers (although He desires them). It's *Jeff* who needs Jeff's prayers! Praying is for us—it's our mode to come into a real relationship with God. Consider this: God Almighty Himself, the Maker of heaven and earth, has invited us to experience Him. Each individual. That's pretty amazing! That is a gift to us.

How should we pray?

So when we pray, we experience God. The Bible says, "Ask and it will be given to you; seek and you will find; knock and the door will be opened to you" (Luke 11:9). Praying helps us know who God is, invest into a relationship with Him, discover His will, and discern right choices.

How much should you pray? The Bible says to "pray continually" (1 Thessalonians 5:17 NASB). This means we must always have an attitude of prayer and strive to make it a priority every day.

Prayer is simply talking and listening to God. So why not start a conversation with Him today? He's God. He can hear you when you talk aloud, He can hear your prayers even as you think thoughts to Him in silence, and He wants to hear from you. (Not just in emergencies, either!)

iThink

1. When does praying come easy and when is it difficult?

_____

_____

_____

2. Something I'd like to confess to God is: _____

_____

_____

_____

3. My top two prayer requests are: _____

_____

_____

_____

4. Spend some time in prayer right now using the ACTS

method. _____

_____

_____

Check here if you believe God is more than
a spiritual 911 operator.

iBelieve in Time Alone with God

In seventh grade, I left home on a week-long trip for the first time in my life. Destination: summer camp. Summer camp was a big deal at my church. Every August, hundreds of squirrelly junior higher kids loaded onto big, old, blue school buses and traveled to a camp situated on a lake so beautiful it was actually named Lake Beauty!

Summer camp was full of firsts for me. It was my first time playing night games in the woods, my first experience taking the polar bear plunge into an icy cold lake at sunrise, and my first experience breaking a bone. (In the middle of the second night of camp, I rolled off my top bunk and fell face first onto the concrete floor six feet below. Luckily, my nose broke my fall.)

I remember one other first that week of summer camp. It was the first time I heard about spending "time alone with God"—our leaders called it TAWG. Each morning that week, the camp leaders had us take our Bibles to a place where we could spend time alone with God before the busyness of camp life resumed.

TAWG seemed strange at first, but the more I did it the more I understood what I was really doing. TAWG is nothing more than time set aside to focus on your relationship with God. We are to "grow...in the knowledge of our Lord and Savior Jesus Christ" (2 Peter 3:18). Spending time in the Bible and praying are sure ways to know Jesus more.

The Time crunch

Perhaps the biggest challenge to spending time alone with God is making the time. Nick gave himself a challenge to set aside ten minutes a day when he started spending TAWG.

Nick found a few easy ways to work in time with God:
- he woke ten minutes earlier than usual
- he gave up ten minutes on the internet
- he spent TAWG even before he crawled out of bed
- he showered at night so he wouldn't be so rushed in the morning

But Nick, a busy student, said the best plan for him was just to find a consistent time each day and stick with it. (This is what serious athletes say about their training schedules, too.) Consistency is the key, even if that means giving up a few minutes of computer time during your day.

The zone

People talk about getting in "the zone" a lot. For athletes, musicians, students, artists, writers, and video-game junkies, getting in the zone means finding concentration and drive to be at their best. It means tuning out all other distractions so they can focus on just one thing.

Do you want to be at your best when you spend TAWG? The environment around you can help or hurt your ability to get in the zone. Some people need total silence, while others like to play music in the background to concentrate. Usually a private space helps keep distractions from creeping in. Wherever you go, make sure it is comfortable and allows for your full concentration.

The Big question

You may wonder "What do I do once I am alone with God?" Praying and reading from the Bible will give you insight into God's plan for your life. The Bible has sixty-six books in the Old and New Testaments. A good place to begin for many is the book of Proverbs.

Proverbs has thirty-one chapters, making it easy to read one each day of the month. And it's the book of wisdom—who couldn't use a little wisdom every day?

Wherever you begin in your Bible reading, you might ask yourself these questions:

- What's something new I learned from God's Word today?
- What's one of God's truths that is good to remember today?

There's no set way to have TAWG, but it's the foundation of your relationship with God. As we've seen in earlier chapters, relationships take time. Can you make time for TAWG? Give it a try for one week and see if you feel closer to God.

iThink

Goals worth reaching are goals worth writing down.

1. I will spend _____ minutes each day in TAWG this week.

2. The best time of the day for me to set aside is: _____

3. A good space for me to be alone and undistracted is:

_____

_____

_____

4. I want to read from the Book of _____ this week.

_____

_____

_____

_____

_____

_____

_____

_____

_____

_____

_____

_____

Check here if you believe in spending time alone with God every day.

WEEK3//DAY3
STILL SMALL VOICE

iBelieve I can Hear God's voice

Moms don't always speak softly, sometimes they yell. Great moms often scream. Knowing that their children's ears have built-in plugs to block out noises that sound like "stop," or "come here," they simply amplify their volume. A lot. Kathy, a mom of two teenage sons, jokingly says, "The meaner the mom, the better the kid." In her house, even the dog yells. But it could be argued that if you really want a child's attention, just whisper something to someone else. That never seems to fail to get them to listen.

The Holy Spirit, the part of God that speaks to your conscience, speaks with a "still small voice" that's easy to miss if we're not intently seeking it. God doesn't like to compete for our attention. He doesn't like to bully or yell. He simply whispers. The more times we tune it out, however, the harder it is to hear the next time.

God will reveal everything we need through the Holy Spirit. But still, many Christians live empty, unfulfilled, and spiritually shallow lives. They live only by what they understand on their own, instead of tapping into the Holy Spirit who sees a complete picture. They fail to listen to the still small voice.

The Key

The Holy Spirit lives in every Christian and longs to help us understand and apply God's Word (John 16:13). He is to a Christian what GPS is to an automobile driver—a guide. More specifically, the Holy Spirit is our guide to truth.

When we use phrases like "filled with anger" or "overcome with grief," what we are really saying is that those emotions control the person. Instead, we should be under the control of the Holy Spirit. That is the key. He will guide us where we need to go.

one or the other

The Holy Spirit will never leave a Christian, but to be filled—or controlled—is another matter. When you grab the steering wheel back, just like turning off the GPS and trying to navigate without a guide, you're on your own.

We really only have two choices for each decision we make: to do things God's way or another way. So we choose between:

- Being filled with the Holy Spirit or being drunk.
- Being filled with the Holy Spirit or loosing your temper.
- Being filled with the Holy Spirit or experiencing sexual sin.
- Being filled with the Holy Spirit or cheating.
- Being filled with the Holy Spirit or gossiping.
- Being filled with the Holy Spirit or lying.
- Being filled with the Holy Spirit or (fill in the blank)

_____

One way to tune out the Holy Spirit is to sin against God.
Making a decision to sin is the same as telling the Holy Spirit
to butt out while we steer the ship.

Bottom line: it's not possible to choose sin and be controlled
by the Holy Spirit at the same time. It's one or the other.
Being controlled by the Holy Spirit is totally up to you.
It's your choice.

Draw Near

The Bible says when we draw near to God He will come
near to us (James 4:8). That means that when we turn
away from sin and set our eyes and hearts on living for
God, we actually pull ourselves into a more intimate, closer
relationship with Him.

It's so much easier to hear a whisper at close range than
from a distance. The still small voice of God—the Holy Spirit
that lives in every Christian—is speaking. We need only to
draw near enough to hear Him.

1. Describe a time when you've felt "filled" with an emotion that controlled you. Was that helpful or hurtful? _____

_____

_____

_____

_____

2. How is it impossible to be filled with the Holy Spirit and sin against God at the same time? _____

_____

_____

_____

_____

_____

3. What's stopping you from drawing nearer to God today?

_____

_____

_____

_____

4. What's keeping you from hearing God's voice? _____

_____

_____

_____

_____

_____

_____

_____

_____

_____

_____

_____

_____

_____

_____

_____

_____

⬤ Check here if you believe God is talking to you in a still small voice.

WEEK3//DAY4
200 HAMBURGERS

Greg is a typical student with one twist. When many other college students frequent frat parties or bars, Greg feeds homeless men at a shelter in the inner city.

Every Tuesday night he packs and delivers two hundred McDonald's double cheeseburgers. His kindness and genuine care often open doors to conversations about God with the people he serves.

To pay for the food, Greg runs a "dollar campaign," each week challenging students at his college to contribute one dollar. One dollar goes a long way at McDonald's—often it buys a double cheeseburger.

Greg and his friends didn't want to wait until they graduated to serve—they are doing it right now. Serving is simply using the gifts God has given you to put another's needs before your own.

Blessed to Be a Blessing

Greg's double cheeseburger idea was a great one. How many of us would have thought of it? It is simple, yet unique. What creative way can you think of to serve others?

Serving is a privilege. Jesus Himself came to serve, and tells us to follow His example. What you'll find, as you begin to serve others, is that you usually receive more blessings than you give. It's amazing.

I mentor young people and invest my time, money, and talent in them almost daily. But the more I do that, the richer my life becomes. In many cases, the people I serve teach me more than I teach them. They become little brothers, sisters, and extended family. They keep the smile on my face.

YOUr TUrn

You can start serving today. Even if you're a broke student like Greg, you have something special to share with others: YOURSELF! Be creative. Serving does not need to cost tons of money—it could be as simple as sharing your words, time, or energy with others. You will receive as much as you give. You'll receive satisfaction in thinking of someone else. You will also receive blessings from the Lord for sharing love in His name.

"God works through the people I serve to bless me in return. It feels uneven, like I get far more back than I ever give."

To find creative, practical ways to help others, try answering the following questions. It's okay to have more than one answer for each question:

- What is your favorite age/people group (outside of your close friends)? Do you enjoy visiting with senior citizens, playing with little children, helping people who don't speak English?
- Would you rather be outdoors, indoors, up early, up late, in a big group, independent, behind the scenes, or out in front?
- Are there specific talents that you've received compliments for? Are you athletic, musical, organized, handy with tools, a good listener, or funny? Do you have a green thumb, bake yummy cookies, or draw awesome pictures?

Based on your answers to the questions above, what is one creative way you could put someone else's needs before your own in the next twenty-four hours?

As you begin to share your gifts and talents by serving others, you will begin to experience the great joy of ministry.

Now, off to it!

ithink

1. How does serving someone open the door to share your faith? _____

_____

_____

_____

_____

2. Tell about a meaningful time when someone served you? How did you feel about that person and about yourself afterward? _____

_____

_____

_____

_____

3. How is serving someone else really serving God? _____

_____

_____

_____

_____

_____

4. Think of five creative ways to serve another person or group for under five dollars. _____

_____

_____

_____

_____

_____

_____

_____

_____

_____

_____

_____

_____

_____

_____

_____

_____

● Check here if you believe you can serve God by serving others.

iBelieve in sharing my faith

It would be hard to find two students who were more popular at school than Dan and Amanda. One was homecoming king, the other class president. Both were star athletes and captains of their teams. They had tremendous influence at their school. And they knew it.

These two, along with their friends, wore t-shirts to school that read, "Do you agree with Dan and Amanda?" Posters hung in the hallways and lunchroom with the same message.

The posters also announced a special after-school assembly. Students would have to attend the assembly to find out what they might be agreeing with. Hundreds came. Then, Dan and Amanda shared their faith in Jesus Christ. They put their reputations on the line because they know hell is hot and eternity is long. After telling their stories, they asked the students if they agreed.

A Burden for Others

To understand how important it is to share Christ with unbelievers, we must remember the stakes involved. It's *literally* a matter of life and death.

Some people will spend eternity separate from Jesus in a horrible place called hell, because they chose to reject Him. Others haven't heard the truth of Jesus yet. This stark reality should not only compel Christians to share their faith, it should strike a sense of urgency in each believer.

The Bible asks three tough questions in Romans 10:14 (THE MESSAGE):

1. How can people call for help if they don't know who to trust?
2. How can they know who to trust if they haven't heard of the One who can be trusted?
3. How can they hear if nobody tells them?

The three questions above are tough because they put a lot of responsibility on us. It's up to Christians to share the hope that is inside them with the rest of the world. The message has to go out that each person is hopelessly lost without a personal relationship with Jesus. It's up to us to "go and make disciples" (Matthew 28:19).

Your story

Most people are experts at talking about themselves. But at the same time, most Christians are silent when it comes to sharing their faith with unsaved friends.

Perhaps the most intimidating part of talking about Jesus is knowing what to say. Take a cue from Dan and Amanda and just share your story. Share how Jesus has impacted your life. Nobody can dispute or reject your experiences. Be bold and courageous!

People tell stories of their experiences all the time. We've all heard stories about:
- the big fish that got away
- parents who walked to school uphill each way
- hookups and breakups (sadly)

Beautiful Feet

Consider your feelings about the person who shared Christ with you—pretty good, right? Romans 10:15 says, "How beautiful are the feet of those who bring good news." It's a privilege to be part of God's plan in someone else's life. It's an honor to be the beautiful feet that bring good news. Do you agree?

1. How do you feel about the person who brought you into a personal relationship with Jesus? _____

_____

_____

_____

_____

2. Name three people to which you'll share your faith story with. _____

_____

_____

_____

_____

3. What's the worst that could happen if you share your faith with those three people? How can you prepare for that? _____

_____

_____

_____

_____

4. How would you share your faith in 30 seconds? (Hint:

make it personal—just tell your story.) ———————

———————————————————————

———————————————————————

———————————————————————

———————————————————————

———————————————————————

———————————————————————

———————————————————————

———————————————————————

———————————————————————

———————————————————————

———————————————————————

———————————————————————

———————————————————————

———————————————————————

———————————————————————

———————————————————————

Check here if you believe you have a responsibility
to share your faith.

DEVOTIONS

WEEK FOUR

FOR REAL LIFE

hat I believe about the Heavy side of faith

Next time you hear someone say, "Go to hell!" you may
think differently about those words. You probably already
know such a phrase is mean-spirited. But when you choose
to believe what the Bible says about hell, you wouldn't
even want your worse enemy in the world to go there.
It's that bad.

Hell is just one of the topics in Week Four. You can't come to know what you believe about God and the Christian life without facing the heavy side of faith head-on. You just can't get around it.

Is hell real? Who is Satan? What about really bad people? Why do they deserve forgiveness? What if I'm just not sure about it all? How can I get to heaven? These are some deep topics. But taken one by one, you will get a good idea of the facts and be able to come to some conclusions about what you believe is true.

The Devil is real and he hates you. In hell, you're always dying but never dead. Even good people go to hell. These are hard truths. Perhaps the toughest idea to swallow, however, is the idea of forgiving the people who hurt you the most. No doubt, you have experienced pain in your life because of what another person has said or done to you. In Nolan's story, you'll read about two loving parents who forgave the man who killed their son. How could they do that? What does their story of forgiveness mean to you?

As you near the end of *iBelieve*, you have probably found answers to some of your questions and probably more questions. On some topics, you may have developed a clearer idea of what you believe. On others, you may have doubts. This week you'll read that doubt is not the opposite of faith—it's an ingredient in faith! So go ahead and question. God gives us the faith needed to overcome doubt.

The last chapter of Week Four will explore how to know God personally. It's a decision only you can make.

Do you believe in new life in Christ? This just may be the time to start standing up for what you believe.

WEEK4//DAY1
KNOW YOUR ENEMY

There is a dog on my street that hates me. Every night when I take a walk or jog through the neighborhood, Killer waits for me at the edge of his yard. And every night, he scares me half to death. If not for the electric fence that zaps him under control, I think he'd chew me to pieces! I'm convinced he hates me.

satan Hates You

Somebody hates you more than that dog hates me. It is the Devil himself, and he is dangerous. He hates you eternally.

It's not enough to just know his name—it's critical to understand the way he works. That is the only way we can prepare ourselves for his attacks.

on the prowl

The Bible says Satan "prowls around like a roaring lion looking for someone to devour" (1 Peter 5:8). It's not enough for Satan to simply hate you—he wants to ruin your life. His ways are predictable, but clever. He has a knack for searching out your biggest vulnerability and attacking there.

Satan is called by many different names in the Bible. Here are just a few:
- the Enemy
  (1 Peter 5:8)
- the Evil One
  (Matthew 13:19)
- the Father of Lies
  (John 8:44)
- the Tempter
  (1 Thessalonians 3:5)
- the Thief
  (John 10:10)

A thief who wants to break into a house usually starts with the doors. If that doesn't work, he goes through a window. Even dumb burglars know it's easier to enter through openings than to tear through bricks and concrete. Satan is a thief too. He wants to rob you of the peace of God and take away the blessings that are available to you. And he looks for any opening, even a crack, to penetrate your mind with his wicked schemes.

clever Beauty

What's more tempting: a juicy T-bone steak or a chewed up T-bone thrown to the dogs? For anyone who's not vegetarian, the easy answer is the juicy steak. The enemy knows our weaknesses. He can sense our hunger, our cravings. He knows how to disguise himself as mouth-watering goodness when he's really poison to our souls.

A clever enemy, Satan will do his best to allure us with something that looks beautiful but isn't. Pornography is one example of something terrible disguised as something beautiful. Most males, and many females, are attracted to exotic images of physical beauty. But lurking behind the façade of beauty is a deep, dark oppressive danger. The influence of pornography robs a Christian of his or her purity, peace, and intimacy with God and others. Pornography develops sin strongholds and produces life-long battles. It destroys gender respect and self respect. Pornography sells the lie—from the Father of Lies—that it satisfies. Pornography is not beautiful; it is soul-rotting!

anticipate and combat

Any general in the U.S. military will tell you how important it is to anticipate an enemy's plan of attack. Our country spends billions of dollars every year collecting intelligence on our enemies around the world. With a good idea of the enemy's strategy, the military can best plan its defense to ensure victory. Where will the Devil likely tempt you today? What stronghold or foothold will he cling to in your life? He has done the reconnaissance and knows your weaknesses. It may be a door wide open, a window unlatched, or a crack in a wall, but he's looking to infiltrate you—his enemy.

Anticipate where the enemy is going to attack—and claim that area in your life for the Lord. The first step is accepting that the Devil is real. The second step is preparing for his attacks. Satan has no power over the Christian who puts on the whole armor of God (Ephesians 6:11).

iThink

1. What do the different names of Satan reveal about his nature and mission? _____

_____

_____

_____

_____

2. If Satan gathers secret intelligence on you, what are two areas in your life where he finds the greatest vulnerability to devour you? _____

_____

_____

_____

_____

3. What specific action can you take to prepare for his attack in those two areas? _____

_____

_____

_____

_____

_____

_____

4. Describe a strategy you've seen the Devil use to hurt someone you know (name can remain anonymous). ____

_____

_____

_____

_____

_____

_____

_____

_____

● Check here if you believe Satan is real and is after your soul.

WEEK4//DAY2
GASPING FOR AIR

iBelieve in an Eternal Hell

Little kids love to swim on hot summer days. If one swims a little bit too far away from where he can touch the bottom—just a matter of inches sometimes—a fun, playful moment can quickly turn scary. The feeling of running out of breath under water, unable to come up for air, is one of the worst feelings in the world. The body feels the strain of something missing—the very air we breathe—and every pore screams.

The human body also relies on water to run properly. Every athlete recognizes the importance of maintaining fluids in times of intense exercise. Have you ever worked out so hard and become so thirsty that your thirst actually hurts? Picture a wanderer stuck in the desert without water—hallucinating and weary, almost paralyzed by thirst. That is hurting thirst.

Billy Graham said that no matter how excruciating the fire of hell may be, "the thirst of a lost soul for the Living Water will be more painful." Hell is not what you thought it was as a kid—the playground of a little red devil with a pitchfork where you can indulge in fun activities for all eternity. It is a final and painful separation from God, eternal and irreversible.

A soul forever without God is like a human body forever without oxygen or water. Never-ending suffocation and eternally unsatisfied thirst. Constant agony.

Hell is Torment

A woman recently made headlines after she underwent

would ever wish upon anyone. In the middle of her procedure, her anesthesia wore off and she could feel the pain of the instruments. The biggest problem was that because of another medication at work in her system,

> The Bible describes hell as a place of constant, conscious torment. These verses (as well as others) offer insight on the reality of hell:
>
> > "furnace of fire…weeping and gnashing of teeth" (Matthew 13:50 NASB)
> >
> > "where their worm does not die, and the fire is not quenched" (Mark 9:48 NASB)
> >
> > "he will be tormented with fire and brimstone" (Revelation 14:10 NASB)

she was unable to speak or move. For the rest of the surgery, the woman was tormented and tortured—fully aware of the pain, but unable to respond to it or stop it.

The fire of hell may be literal or figurative, but one thing is certain: it is a place of constant, unending suffering and loneliness.

Eternal and Irreversible

Stephen Murray, an X Games gold medal winner in BMX Freestyle competition, was paralyzed from the neck down after a horrific accident during an ESPN-televised competition. Stephen's double backflip gone bad turned into a permanent life-changing injury. Stephen can never redo that jump or take back the consequences of his fall. Hell is an irreversible destination for every one of its inhabitants. Once someone goes to hell, it's for good. Just as Stephen has no redos, an unbeliever who dies and goes to hell can't ever redo his decision to reject Christ. But unlike Stephen's situation, which will affect him for the next 40 years or so (the rest of his earthly life), hell lasts for all eternity. It's an agony that literally never ends.

The Bible describes hell as eternal agony: "The smoke of their torment goes up forever and ever and they have no rest day and night" (Revelation 14:11 NASB).

Revelation 20:14 (NASB) calls hell a second death, because like death on earth, there is no reversing the outcome. In hell, it's never over—you're always dying but never dead.

choice

Basically, hell is banishment from the presence of God once
and for all. It's the outcome for deliberately rejecting Jesus
Christ as Lord and Savior. We have only our lifetime on earth
to make this choice that affects the rest of eternity.

In the book of John, God says He has condemned no one
to hell. People who end up there will have condemned
themselves by rejecting Jesus. We need to accept Jesus
Christ into our lives. It is our choice. When we don't,
we reject Him not only now, but forever.

Once we accept Christ, He gives us the free gift of eternal
life. We need not fear hell because He promises His
followers eternal life in heaven. We can concentrate on
heaven and not worry about hell.

iThink

1. What are some common misconceptions about hell? ___

_____

_____

_____

2. What's one idea from this chapter that you have not considered before now? _____

_____

_____

3. What's the one deciding factor in whether a person goes to heaven or hell? _____

_____

_____

4. Knowing how awful hell is, what keeps some people from turning to Jesus for eternal life in heaven? Is anything keeping you from Jesus? _____

_____

_____

_____

_____

_____

_____

●   Check here if you believe hell is a real place.

WEEK4//DAY3
NOLAN

The fall of Nolan's freshman year in college was filled with new experiences. In the first two months of the term, Nolan quickly made friends with dozens of guys and girls. Life in college was going well for Nolan—then tragedy struck.

On the way to a Halloween party, Nolan and two friends pulled to the side of the road to assist stranded motorists involved in a car accident. What began as a Good Samaritan–effort turned into the deadliest traffic accident in Wake County in over twenty years. As Nolan pulled an injured motorist out of a truck, another vehicle driven by a drunk driver raced through the intersection and into the crowd of pedestrians on the side of the road. Nolan and four others were killed instantly—another died later that night and two others were severely injured.

Nolan's parents lost their only son. They never had a chance to say "good-bye" or "I love you" one last time. His sister lost her only brother. The entire incident was avoidable if Larry, the drunken motorist, had made better choices that night.

Forgive others...for their sake

Larry carried enormous guilt and suffered deeply for his crime. Just like all of the loved ones involved, it was difficult for Larry to move on from his mistake and begin living again. Depressed and despised by others, it would have been easy for him to rot away in his prison cell and never make a positive contribution to society again.

A year after his death, Nolan's dad wrote a letter to the man who killed his son. Sitting in his prison cell, Larry read the words that changed his life: "[I] forgive you for taking Nolan's life." Nolan's mom and dad went one step further: they took the remainder of Nolan's college fund and set it aside to pay for Larry's rehabilitation. It was time to begin healing.

The forgiveness Larry experienced profoundly impacted his life. Through the forgiveness of Nolan's family, he knew that God forgave him too. He asked Jesus to come into his life and he started following hard after God. He started reaching others for Christ with his powerful testimony. Today, he serves as an inmate chapel leader in prison, helping other criminals come to find forgiveness from God.

God will Forgive...and Forget

It is possible to fly a plane headed east, circle the globe, and be pointed east all along the way. East never ends because it never touches west. God says He will forgive our sins as far as the east is from the west. That means God's forgiveness is unending—without limit. There is nothing too big for God to forgive.

Have you ever forgiven someone, but then continued to remember how much he or she hurt you? In the book of Isaiah, God says that He "remembers your sins no more" (43:25). God will not only forgive the sins of His children, He'll actually banish those sins from His memory. God, who knows everything, chooses to forget that which He has forgiven! It's a clean start and a promise you can believe—because He said it, and it's impossible for Him to lie (Hebrews 6:18).

Forgive others…for your sake

The story of Nolan's death and the example of his parents' forgiveness is tremendous. Most parents couldn't imagine forgiving such a crime, but Nolan's mom and dad realized

Tips on Forgiving Yourself:
- Make a decision to move forward—a change of direction from the mistake.
- Confess your sin to God if you're genuiely sorry—God WILL forgive you.
- Trust God for forgiveness—agree with God that you are forgiven.
- Remember that grace is undeserved favor—give yourself lots of grace.

they didn't have a choice if they wanted to fully experience God's grace in their own lives. Nolan's parents found it within their hearts to forgive the most unforgivable offense any parent could endure, because they knew that God has forgiven them. They forgave the man who killed their son so they could move on with the life God had planned for them.

Tips on Forgiving Someone Else:
- Remember that we forgive out of love and obedience to God—failing to forgive someone else is actually sinning against God.
- Know that forgiveness is even more beneficial for the person doing the forgiving than it is for the person being forgiven.
- Ask God for help when it's tough to forgive.

Satan would love nothing more than to cripple our lives with hatred and bitterness. As we hold to those feelings and withhold forgiveness, we actually lose more of our lives to the "thief." Forgiveness is as much for us as it is for the person being forgiven. We are called by God to forgive others just as He has forgiven us.

1. Describe a time when you've experienced forgiveness from someone else. _____

_____

_____

2. Describe a time when you've experienced forgiveness from God. _____

_____

_____

3. Describe a time when it was really tough to forgive someone else. _____

_____

_____

4. Is there anyone in your life you need to forgive...for their sake, and for yours? _____

_____

_____

_____

Check here if you believe forgiveness is necessary for yourself and others.

iBelieve Doubt is okay with God

Kevin believed in God, but it freaked him out every time he had doubts. One time, it seemed impossible to Kevin that God could hear his prayers. Another time, he had questions about how to know for sure that the Bible is God's Word. Whenever he was skeptical about God, he felt bad about questioning his faith. He worried that maybe his doubt was sin.

Doubts are the question marks that punctuate our beliefs. God asks for our faith, but not blind faith. It's okay to have questions and search for answers.

Faith is a choice

C. S. Lewis once said that doubt is not the opposite of faith—it is a necessary ingredient. If there was no element of doubt, there would be no room for faith (it would just be fact).

Besides operating the remote control and plugging the cord into the outlet, how my television works to create what I see on the screen is beyond me. But I don't need a technology genius to explain every step of broadcast science to believe that when I turn on my TV, I will see pictures and hear sound. I learn some of the facts and choose to take the rest on faith. God will reveal Himself to you through the Bible and your prayers. But no matter how many questions are answered, you'll always think of one more. At some point, you will need to choose to believe—even without all the answers.

YOU Have Faith!

Every sip of water from the faucet is an act of faith that involves trusting that the water is drinkable and safe. Each act of sitting down on a chair takes faith—trusting it to hold you and not break. What would a walk through your house reveal about the things you accept by faith every day?

Fill in the blanks below with something you accept by faith in each room.

Kitchen _____

Bathroom _____

Bedroom _____

Living room _____

Car _____

Faith-Busters

Without faith it is impossible to please God (Hebrews 11:6). Besides natural curiosity, there are three *faith-busters* to avoid or eliminate from your life:

- Deliberate sin. A season of deliberate sin affects a

Christ-follower's faith like a drought affects a field of crops. In the presence of sin, faith withers away.

- Absence of truth. To know the Scriptures is to spot the Enemy's lies. Since the Garden of Eden, Satan has lied to create doubt in the hearts of Christians. Without God's Word in our hearts there is more room for Satan's deceptions.

- Lack of effort. Isolation from other believers can cast a cloud of doubt over anyone. But engaging in ministry, participating in worship, and being part of a Christian community all bring faith alive.

Instead of seeing doubt as something bad, think of it as an opportunity to flex your faith muscles and grow even stronger.

1. Which faith-buster causes the most problems in your life: deliberate sin, absence of truth, or lack of effort? ____

_____

_____

_____

_____

2. What's one thing about your Christian faith that you sometimes doubt? _____

_____

_____

_____

_____

3. The Bible is your complete guide—what are two verses that speak to your area of doubt? (This might take some digging.) _____

_____

_____

_____

_____

4. Share one of your doubts with someone you trust—maybe it's something they have wrestled through and can understand. _____

_____

_____

_____

_____

_____

_____

_____

_____

_____

_____

_____

_____

_____

_____

_____

○ Check here if you believe doubting God and the Bible is part of faith.

WEEK4//DAYS
FOREVER

iBelieve I'm eternal

When you wake up each morning, what is your first thought?
Is it the looming deadline of a class project or maybe that
special somebody you like? If you're like me, you wish you
could sleep a few more minutes! No matter what your waking
thoughts may be, or how dreary or exciting your days may
look, in the grand scheme of things, what is important to
remember is that you are eternal.

Our time on earth is short. But this is not all there is. What does it mean to have eternal life, and how do we get it?

what is eternal life?

As I write this book, I am suffering an incurable fate. I am dying. In fact, you are too. There is not a person on earth who will not die. Today, the odds are that we will have about eighty years on this rock, give or take a few. My dentist says people who floss their teeth live longer—in that case, it's not looking so good for me.

Eternity is a long time. Imagine a bird whose job it is to move the entire West Coast beach to the East Coast, one grain at a time. The poor bird needs to clasp one grain in his mouth and fly thousands of miles only to turn around and come back for the next grain, over and over and over. When he finally delivers the last grain of sand, he finds out that he needs to bring each one back to the West Coast, one at a time. How many thousands of years would that take? Now consider this: after the bird finally returns the last grain of sand to the beach where he began, *eternity has not even begun.* Eternity is unending, so each day it is literally just beginning.

Eternal life is the part of life that begins as soon as life on earth ends. Eternal life is nonnegotiable and unavoidable. Everyone will live forever...we just need to determine where.

who Has Eternal Life in Heaven?

In movies, heaven is located on a bed of white, fluffy clouds, and everyone goes there unless they were really bad on earth. But that image of heaven is as cartoonish as a nursery rhyme or Disney story.

Heaven is a place God has prepared for Christ-followers to spend eternity. For Christians—people who follow Jesus Christ as the Lord of their lives—it's a place where we will come into the presence of our Savior. Heaven is perfect and without sin, and that's why we can't get there on our own. Jesus says in the gospel of John that no man or woman comes to God except through Him (John 14:6). Jesus came to earth to die for all of our sins so that anyone who calls on

His name will have eternal life in heaven. His death covers our sin. It is a free gift. But like any other gift, we need to accept it before it becomes our own. How do you do that?

As we learned in Week One, all you have to do is ask Jesus into your life. In your own words:

- thank God for sending His Son Jesus to die for your sins.
- admit you are a sinner living a sinful life.
- ask Jesus to come into your life and forgive your sins right now.
- acknowledge Jesus is the only way to become right with God.
- ask Jesus to take control of your life.
- tell Jesus you believe He's in you and will never leave you.

what Happens to everyone else?

Bad people who don't know Jesus—unrepentant murderers, adulterers, thieves, and rapists—go to hell. But so do good people who don't know Jesus! Hell will be populated with pastors, priests, food-shelf volunteers, teachers, doctors, grandparents, and others who have rejected Jesus. What might sound like a bleak message doesn't need to scare you. The good news is that everyone—no matter who—has the same opportunity to know that God is calling out to them. Everyone has a choice to believe that Jesus died to give eternal life. And everyone who calls on the name of Jesus will find eternal life. It's all about following up on

iThink

1. How would you describe eternity to someone? _____

_____

_____

_____

_____

2. What one decision impacts whether a person will spend eternity in heaven or hell? _____

_____

_____

_____

_____

3. What does it mean to be a Christian? _____

_____

_____

_____

_____

_____

4. How secure do you feel about your eternal destiny?

Why? _____

_____

_____

_____

_____

_____

_____

_____

_____

_____

● Check here if you believe your life is eternal.

- iBelieve I am a child of God.
- iBelieve God loves me unconditionally.
- iBelieve I am one of God's masterpieces.
- iBelieve pride is something I should fight against.
- iBelieve I am a Christian.
- iBelieve I should fear God.
- iBelieve godly relationships are necessary.
- iBelieve my "stuff" belongs to God.
- iBelieve I should be obedient to God.
- iBelieve God provides a way out of tough situations.
- iBelieve God is more than a spiritual 911 operator.
- iBelieve in spending time alone with God every day.
- iBelieve God is talking to me in a still small voice.
- iBelieve I can serve God by serving others.
- iBelieve I have a responsibility to share my faith.
- iBelieve Satan is real and is after my soul.
- iBelieve hell is a real place.
- iBelieve forgiveness is necessary for myself and others.
- iBelieve doubting God and the Bible is part of faith.
- iBelieve my life is eternal.

Much like *iBelieve*, the companion volume *iChoose* will guide you through real life issues and choices. Let it help you find the courage to stand up for what you believe in.